D0722863

Unsleeping

Also by Michael Burkard

In a White Light 1979

None, River 1979

Some Time in the Winter (chapbook) 1979

Ruby for Grief 1981

The Fires They Kept 1986

Fictions from the Self 1988

My Secret Boat 1990

*My Brother Makes a Toast but Uses
by Mistake His Name* (chapbook) 1992

Three (chapbook) 1997

Entire Dilemma 1998

Pennsylvania Collection Agency 2001

UNSLEEPING

POEMS

MICHAEL BURKARD

Sarabande Books

LOUISVILLE, KENTUCKY

FIRST EDITION

No part of this book may be reproduced without written permission of the publisher.
Please direct inquiries to:

Managing Editor
Sarabande Books, Inc.
2234 Dundee Road, Suite 200
Louisville, KY 40205

LIBRARY OF CONGRESS CATALOGING-IN-PUBLICATION DATA
Burkard, Michael, 1947–
    Unsleeping : poems / by Michael Burkard.— 1st ed.
    p. cm.
    ISBN 1-889330-52-3 (cloth: alk. paper) — ISBN 1-889330-53-1 (pbk: alk. paper)
I. Title.
PS3552.U718 U57 2001
811'.54—dc21   00-030130

Cover image: *Camera Obscura Image of Houses Across the Street in Our Bedroom*, 1991
by Abelardo Morell. Provided courtesy of Bonni Benrubi Gallery, NYC.

Cover and text design by Charles Casey Martin.

Manufactured in Canada.
This book is printed on acid-free paper.

Sarabande Books is a nonprofit literary organization.

Funded in part by a grant from the Kentucky Arts Council, a state agency of the
Education, Arts, and Humanities Cabinet, and by a grant from the National
Endowment for the Arts.

for Charlie Bagley

Acknowledgments

Grateful acknowledgment is made to the editors of the following publications in which some of the poems in this book first appeared: *The American Poetry Review, Barrow Street, Hayden's Ferry Review, Heliotrope, The Louisville Review, Magazine of the Arts* (SUNY Purchase), *The Plum Review, Salt Hill Journal, Skyline,* and *3rd Bed.*

The epigraph by Federico García Lorca, "Romance Sonámbulo" ("Sleepwalking Ballad"), is from *Selected Poems,* © 1955 New Directions Publishing Corp.

Contents

TWO

Romance Sonámbulo

Pero yo ya no soy yo,
ni mi casa es ya mi casa.

Sleepwalking Ballad

But now I am not I,
nor is my house now my house.

—Federico García Lorca
translated by Nancy Modlin Katz

/ indicates a stanza break lost in pagination

UNSLEEPING

ONE

Harlem

Two copies of Denis Johnson's
Jesus' Son, write *song* instead.
The way the woman has her hand
up to the back of her head and
what with me without my glasses
her gloves look like they could
be brief eyes. The man with her
doesn't want to write, I assume,
but maybe he would read one of
these if I walk up and in a non-
worrisome way tell myself to be
a lyric or a phrase or a brain
and bring my hand up as in a dream
ends do. Sea-light is my vacant
lot among these evening buildings.
Everyone to do. Love you are like
a mile in the day-sky which has
just shut down. Love I bring home
one book to you from a blue car
from somewhere.

Hat Angel

What could she say? Little money,

little chance for work, a drunk for

a husband she no longer loved,

and now she leaves her winter hat

on the train. Trains feel vast.

Devon's room—not so vast. But it

doesn't move, so she's sitting

there before he comes home smashed

and angry, or maybe he will just

fall down. She reads a few pages

of a book half-backwards. A

hopeless attempt to snap to, to

have something in this life pull

her out of this, like the moon,

the moon's a puller. Like the train:

the train's a puller of forgetfulness

and power and destination far into

the reaches of the forests. What

could she say? Oh she can talk to

herself, but now she's got to get

out, and words won't do this. Al-

most as if words make you stay more.

She doesn't even have a hat to reach

for so can she make the door? Oh

prayer for the hat to be a puller

for her even as it circles the city

or enters someone else's flat, hat
have an arm to keep her from his fist,
moon and train, moon and train, moon
and train: pull her, pull her, pull her.

Erotic Life-Thoughts

Any leads on the broken window?

Any way now to know the answer to your life?

Any weight, any answer?

Any fortune in store as cheap as the one you just read?

Any semicolon the bird would eat from your hand?

A fairy tale with a bridge leading to a penis?

A gingerbread house where the leaves were stone green?

Any solution to the *mast of stone green poem*?

Any cool coin you could grab for again as a boy or a girl?

Any sexual identity which shifted again when you knew

      the forest began but you could not get yourself

      to tell the snow or the thaw?

A fairy tale with a bridge leading to a broken window?

Any room for Tomas' night-book on the table?

A green stone which reflected cheap fortunes back to the sun?

An old house which is large and is the answer to the letter *Z*?

Any trees which resulted in a conspiracy?

Any eats?

Any daylight word?

Today's Crisis

Today's crisis is entitled "Sunlight."
It feels too strict in its brightness.
And upon awakening from a night of ghosts
you feel the brightness is, in a word, opaque.

Solution? In a word: flee!
No, Michael, this will not do.
The dream of ghosts leaves you empty again.
Not as empty as you think,

but empty enough. You followed
your sister down a hill. Your brother
followed also, a slightly minor figure,
perhaps because you were dreaming him

Michael, because, at least last night,
they were not his ghosts, but yours.
You followed after your sister,
she existed and led as some Pied Piper,

but wearing a mask. In fact, if you
look more closely the three of you
were each wearing a mask. The sun
shone upon the hill, but not as

a crisis. The crisis is now, Michael,
you begin the day with that sense,
it encloses you on the one hand
like a rose which has no scent—

and they are producing them you know,
roses which have no scent, Michael,
they are forcing the roses faster
and eliminating the scent—

but on the other hand the crisis
encloses you like the color of the robin,
the robin chirping in the night
beside your sister, just one of the robin's

eyes masked, a half mask, like a tender
joke your sister understood.
"We were meant to be alike, Michael!
We were meant to be alike!"

In the unique arrangement
of a dream, is it not true
a dream is often telling you
you are not "unique"? And, Michael,

is the dream not reaching out
to you? So often you think

it is the other way around—
Michael is reaching out to the dream!,

Michael, fragile Michael, is seeking
a solution, an answer, the hand
of a ghost. You are
the hand of a ghost.

You are a half mask.
You are the rose which still
smells like a rose.
You are "alike."

Today's crisis is entitled "Sunlight."
The dream reaches for you.
Your sister is here with you,
but is nowhere to be found.

Unappreciated Spider

When the construction of such other sobbing starts

When the quietness is both dim and fail dim and fail

When the remembering is you against a you you do not recall

When the unappreciated spider returns to her window just as a reminder

The Thanker

here he was,
this wonderful but awkward poet
thanking another awkward but wonderful poet
for the latter poet's translations
of still another poet—

these blessings were sincere,
one story writer to another,
but as the weeks went by he felt
a genuine need to thank the writer
again, and he did, and again, and he did,

and it was always in a hallway,
and (honestly) there was always
just a little snow, just a little,
falling to earth as he looked behind
the writer's short shoulder to the 6th floor
window—

and by the third or fourth profuse
thank you even the snow was getting tired
of this, and the thanker began to feel
embarrassed—for what or for whom he
was not sure—

but each time he saw the writer

(and he seldom saw the writer, which

made it all the worse)

he had to thank him again not for his

the writer's poems but for

these translations—he looks around,

the thanker, and he snows snow, and the

wonderful but lonely poems the writer wrote.

You could never tell one identity from

another, well that suggests a lack of clarity,

what I am getting at is the writer/

translator was very good at...

and I don't want to suggest that.

The writer wrote very clearly, mysteriously,

—honesty, loneliness, snow, these were almost

virtues underneath the surface of the writer's writing.

The Dandelions

One year the dandelions decided to play a game:
Let's fool that guy who has quit his job into thinking
we are rejoicing with him. And the man drove through the
hills with much insight indeed, and much inside of him.
The constellations of dandelions danced their dances.

Almost to the day a decade later he accidentally or
coincidentally or dandeliondentally is retracing his steps
—his heart of hearts has told him something he has now
slightly confused about being able to reverse the past
by tracing it over or redoing it with intent

—and the dancing is careful to only take place inside
of him, in order to not deplete himself soon, so soon
the whole thing will go up in smoke. Like many of the days
of his life. Like many days during which the dandelions
were rejoicing but, let's face it, no one cared to join.

Or plot the plot.
Or break the break.
Or sign the heart,
like the sea supplying food although it is killed over and over.

Radius of a Ghost

The numbers between 22 and 27
are missing. The child is missing.
The day the child failed geometry
is missing. The day the child stole
his first jeep is missing. The evening
the child broke is not only not
missing, it consists of numbers
and sub-numbers—but I'm not
listening, the sub-number misses someone,
the childish-suddenly of the number—
I am arrested by one ant by a
small pear tree for the first day of
my theft some four decades ago. There
are no witnesses to see. It doesn't
matter. The years numbered between 3
and 23 are missing.

"Foreign" Films

Dr. David could not wait for the night,
whatever that meant. He thought it surprising
I knew he liked foreign films, but all I had done was see
him at a belated Fellini Festival. And I mentioned this
to Dr. David, to him, as half-an-insight. Maybe I even
lied about my half-insight. That would be like me.
To lie. To lie a little. Which turns everything more
on its side than I thought.
"You like foreign films, don't you."
Surprised: "I do. Very much. How
did you know."
"Just a feeling." I hesitate,
but say, "Just a feeling."

Early dark censures our last meeting.
Mr. Me is flunking out of school. Ergo: no more school-
reduced-almost-free visits to school psychiatrist.
Dr. David even stretches to have this one.
The dark is early and clunky and figures to haunt me,
or make Mr. Me sad, or give this crumbly tinge
to much of my crumbly life.

Pictures of the Life

Dear friend J. tells me
M. got used to certain
sets of inexpensive clothing
and always wore them in

photographic or publicity
sessions or openings—
what law or mystery is
involved in this setting

of the ways to keep it
simple—I want to know
but do not ask, and may
have even misheard J.

tell me this—her remarks
and stories are so of interest
I drift slightly enough into
pictures of the life she

is talking toward—need
masks like the kind Magritte's
lovers wear in *The Lovers*
but I don't even know if

they had a choice—even
with their heads covered
they seem closer to love
than I am now. But then

if the face is a window
or if my love is one
I may be a window to their
wounds as well as mine

—and don't forget the
simple slightly dark trees
beyond and the sea there
and clouds and sky

2 Bachelard

We were walking down the street called "I Don't Know" when John turned to me (in a sense turned "on" me) and asked why I had even suggested his art might suffer if he stayed in the city. As soon as the words were coming out of his mouth I felt like, yes, I had made a terrible mistake in saying this, and had crossed some boundary between us which I was conscious of risking, but only conscious of somewhere so still inside myself I could not quite get it yet. But I got what John said and I knew:

days may go by, John will not marry me. We will not sing together on a rainy day as I have hoped. I remembered what Sally had said about Michael: one day I returned from the inner city with two books, one on fire, another on space. Years later I don't have the books—Michael has them I bet—but still have the receipt. 2 Bachelard. Not a street, but two titles by the writer/ thinker/artist-to-my-way-of-thinking Bachelard.

Days do go by. 2 Bachelard begins to feel like a street. I stare at this weak brown slip called a receipt with its clear but incomplete scrawl and an entire world of passion and rain and the inner and outer city returns to me. Yes, a street. A sign. A smell. A love, a life, a love of life when you could not let go of either. When legs opened in the night for love to go between, a true "go-between," but untrue in the end. In another countryside outside another city. Mistakes, heat, hot winds.

But 2 Bachelard. I sense rain. I smell rain. I am getting a cab.

"2 Bachelard."

The Hand

No one knows the honest
end or beginning—no one
knows the important details
—living like this causes
one like her to fold her
hand early, no bluffing
left, and only distracted
ideas as to what's out there.

Why Do You Think the Sea
is So Central to Your Writing?

I don't know. I don't know.
I've never thought much about it.
Now, after the interview, I get
to thinking: it's where we're from,
it's a source . . . it's the source . . .
I don't know . . . I don't know what
I think/think about what I write.
I don't want to know. If I know
I stop. Maybe I want to stop,
to stop this, what has been going
on all these years, what sideways
sea or life am I trying to steer
clear of knowing how deeply it touched
me, how deeply it held me, how deeply
someone took me from this—
I take a card, an overhead view
of Provincetown, showing/emphasizing
the dunes at Provincetown, I take
this card from hundreds of cards
yesterday and keep it out, old
postcard from M. And when I see
it yesterday my stomach or my heart
or something inside and down is
going oh my god don't we miss this
and then today as planned the inter-

viewer calls, and so much of it is
about the sea, and I am so stupid
and lost and in interior New York
State and want to get the hell out
of here. Oh really, deeply, tell
myself slowly.

Back to the Thief

Whom *do* I mean?
On a cold day in Rochester I am thinking of you, it is January, I
am driving through very poor neighborhoods which are truly cold—
you are completely with me at moments but you cannot be the thief.

I make up a song about getting a bad haircut. A very bad haircut.
Maybe I have passed a barber shop or two, or maybe the light of the sun
hits a comma I can't even see on a page on a second floor in a brown
room where a young woman is doing a little looking around.
She may be the thief but do I mean it?

I mean it.
I mean it.
I meant it.

These are simply three red birds attempting to rid themselves of you
as a thief by flying together as the same words almost.

If you were the thief I had perfectly taken the design you had given
me of yourself over the years in constant silence like snow and like
snowfall and like rain and like rainfall.

The sun and the moon and the blue sky and the other sky we knew
about from the beginning.

We did.

We did.

We argued eventually over the actual words of the song and the dream number which assigned itself the song in the juke box.

On a summer day in Rochester I am thinking of you. I am driving through very poor neighborhoods. Some deals look like they are going down. You are completely with me at moments but you cannot be the thief.

Train's Name

Then there is my literal
biological brother who
moved away—take
The Hudson and you can

get there. Permission
is another thing: my
aunts were some of
his favorite people

mine too but they
are gone now glinting
like late fall light
on the river west of

my small window—
who last closed Nellie's
eyes? Who lastly
drinks from the river?

Talking

I am going to tell you he is my brother but he isn't. But there isn't
(is not) any way I am going to talk about what I need to talk about unless
I tell you he is my brother. So I have to start there (here). Talking
is painful, but it feels sometimes as if that is all there ever was, that
it isn't (is not) painful at all.

If I dream of you. I want to go back to sleep.

I never had a friend in childhood whose brain had to be removed. But I
knew of someone by the time I was thirteen or fourteen who had a rare
disease of the brain.

My brother painted. I watched. He gave up painting for one year for
photography (black and white). But when he ran out of subjects (he said
he ran out of subjects) he went back to painting. By this time I was
not watching nearly as much.

I don't know if I have ever dreamed about talking. Just talking. Talking
as the subject for a dream. Although talking could disguise itself as
a subject by, say, being drawing. Space. Drawing space. Disguised
for talking.

My brother is painful sometimes. Coalition.

I tell you he is talking.

Is not.

One time he washed the moon and put it in his pocket. One time he washed the moon and it didn't dry right and it appeared to be all crushed.

Sometimes as if that is all there ever was.

Now you are angry at me and it is pointless to deny the anger. But you are not really angry *at me*. You are angry at *your* brother, or for the fact that I said something to you that would indicate, if only for a second or two, how very close to each other we are, how very close to each other we have always been. And this intimacy is simply something you can't handle. Or *I* can't handle this, but your anger is a disguise *for me*. This would make some sense. We are having one of those Let's-play-unconscious-roles-today-and-trouble-one-another-by-denying-or-moving-through-emotional-life-sideways-Yes.

Three stones from the mountain in France. Three answers hidden on a page in a book.

Your brother's hatred of thick paint. Your brother (not mine).

But I was close to him because he felt to me like he could be the brother I sought.

We misuse words much too often.

/ I can only speak for me.

We threw the moon out. The next night another moon turned up.

When my mother died the nurse told us not to feel we had to hurry to leave her body, that my mother would seem alive/asleep for awhile and that sometimes it was comforting to stay awhile. She would not seem dead right away. And she didn't. Seem dead. And we stayed for what seemed like a minute or two minutes. We did unusual things: I took a photograph and a drawing off of the nursing home wall on her side of the room. We were concerned for her "roommate" who had no legs really and was not ambulatory of course and could not just leave. We thanked her for "being with" my mother, although neither had a choice.

Do I know what my mother thought of my brother or of the moon? Not much.

My mother was terribly uncomfortable with words. Maybe even depressed by them.

Unspeakable Roof

You would have gone nuts too
with the lights flashing around
the walls of the room all night
long. I even see them heading
onto the fourth wall but that
would not make sense—the lights
could not go that far—hey, at
least we had a room, a roof, and
we were much closer to the sky
than most—and we made love to
these lights, before we even knew
what making love was. Face it,
they made love to us, and we,
the two of us out of this ship
in the gigantic world, we made
love back to them. That's one
of many reasons and fortunes
why 1) we never did go nuts
and 2) why the lights still love
us. The walls and the gigantic
world love us too, although often
we think not. The roof too.
The unspeakable roof even loves
us.

for my brother

Rain Trying

Purely, more purely
than night's arc,

the silence of death
converses with objects,

chooses to converse,
near the purity

of night, near
silence of rain,

near silence's
moment after,

near a rain trying
to objectify the earth.

Woodpile

What are you doing without one of these
in your life? Driving by them, they are holding a tree
by what looks like a string—you know it isn't, but this
looks dangerous, because they're not professionals
(you can tell from their clothing), in fact one is
a kid, and thin, and lives only a few doors down
from a house reputed to be a house of domestic
violence. You see the face of your friend Bill yelling
unexpectedly at his child, and you see the face
of Owen chopping away to stay in shape and to
rid himself of excessive anger, so he says. You
are just about to look for a chimney somewhere
farther up the street when you correct a vision
of a distant punishment: you let the unseen bird
continue his early afternoon message, and you
beckon to her from the silent places inside
you never visit frequently enough, or prolonged
enough, so you will be still unless or until
the message stops. You are tired of being afraid
of people, not calling, sounding tonally off.
Thinking too much. You confuse me another says.
You try to explain it is fear and your words
don't seem quite on line. The hell with it.
The tree with it.

talking to a star

but how could you move
again if you wasn't sure
it was time

well it wasn't time but
i had to trust something

what did you trust

a star—do i tell you
about the star

tell me

well one night i was
talking to a star
and just when i ended
another star fell

so you're moving
because a star fell

a few minutes later
another star fell

/
so two stars fall
so what
it's august

it was august

it was august
and two stars fell
—not because you was
talking

not because

so why are you moving

because a star fell
and a few minutes later
another star bit
the sky and fell

33

Kafka Tom

1

Kafka Tom

Kafka train.

Kafka bowl.

Kafka coin.

Kafka leaf.

Kafka kava.

Kafka Sunday.

Kafka de Kooning.

Kafka pond.

Kafka syllable.

Kafka steeple.

Kafka winter.

Kafka heart.

Kafka lie.

Kafka untruth.

Kafka school (Kafka guitar).

Kafka blue.

Kafka whisper.

Kafka period.

Kafka troops.

Don Kafka.

Ordinary Kafka

Broken Kafka.

Pond Kafka.

Kiss Kafka.

Kafka starring Kafka.

Nude Kafka.

Messed up Kafka.

Misspelled Kafka.

Moonlit Kafka.

Tom Kafka.

Chasing Kafka.

Elvis meets Kafka.

Kafka meets Kenneth.

Marilyn meets Kafka.

Kafka meets JoAnn.

Carlos meets Kafka.

Kafka meets Lola.

Lola's twin meets Kafka.

Kafka meets Giannina.

Sex meets Kafka.

Kafka meets the Sex Pistols.

John Skoyles meets Kafka.

Kafka meets Harry, John's son.

And Maria, John's wife.

Kafka does not meet:

Rose

A bonfire

Melissa

Keith

Carlos

A wound

A window with my friend Bob in it

Kafka

Peter Allen

Your dove

Your coffee

Your bullet for so long

"Wedding on a bright clear day"

A summer place, a summer window

Error: Kafka does meet a summer window

Yesterday Kafka boarded the bus

Makes a list of his girlfriends

Makes his bed

Takes awhile to ask my sister about her homework

Takes awhile more to ask me about my grades

Takes awhile more to invite my brother the painter to his opening

Kafka is not a must.

Kafka is not on top.

Kafka is not diffident.

Kafka did not get the job.

Kafka did not get jobbed.

Kafka took my key.

Kafka knew one important collapse opened an original name.

Kafka knew names and earlier names.

2

"Kafka is like a bum jumping off a lyrical bridge but you travel in
a circle to prevent this."

"Kafka is a lonely sky and house beyond it."

"Kafka is to Kafka as a bum is to money."

"Kafka waits until later in the experience of the night."

"When I dream of Kafka I dream of the pronoun 'I'—and 'I' has
a plan."

"Kafka is the story of being told from a still unhappy world."

"Kafka Tom is my dead friend whose ghost gave me his walking stick
recently but was only kidding and asked me to put it near a tree
before I was halfway around the lake and to talk about this only
after a month or so had passed."

Kafka Tom, your shadow is happy and so am I.

I became attached to your shadow, Kafka Tom.

Heartbreak is goodbye for Kafka Tom.

Heartbreak is good for Kafka Tom. We both decided.

3

One time I could not decide anything about Kafka.

He decided me.

If he had not decided me, believe me, I would not and could not

believe in words like "one time," or "yesterday," or "the hill."

Kafka also dressed like the contortions in the river. At the end

of the sky (in praying clothes). But impolite.

Kafka sang "It snowed, it snowed."

One of the times, then more than once, I was sitting at my desk

and the single lamp went out. It was Kafka.

Kafka made me want to write in your apartment in Yonkers.

What a stone that was, what a last love: river ghosts, Kafka.

And the houses were tired of me and Kafka, but we were high enough

to be above the houses, in the trees, as they say, and Kafka loved

this. Partly because he knew it and we would not last.

But we have lasted. It took Kafka a moment to understand this:

Order emptiness and you order me back into your life. I take

orders. Kafka takes orders. I would never have taken them if

I had not silently understood or misunderstood that he took them

too. As the rains began to end and to close, Kafka turned to me

and said something I thought until now was incomplete.

Story of the heart: Kafka's.

Ghost of the past: Kafka's.

No minister, no priest: Kafka's.

When the trees in the wind close: Kafka.

Take a holiday: Kafka.

Answer the door or its sound: Kafka.

When the river knocks: Kafka.

A place, oddly, in the sun, and a house, oddly, by water: Kafka's.

Kafka: take my hand so tightly that I think you are taking it with you.

4

One time I wanted to write about the people I had stolen, the money
I had stolen, the stories I had stolen. I could not find the words
for this book until after Kafka completed me. I don't mean he completed
me as a writer or that I then proceeded to write the book. I wanted
to photograph my teeth at very close range, for their crookedness and
the fact of their smile had been the cause of much tension, tension
which could rearrange entire parts of my life. I was snagged by the utter
smallness of my life. My life had gone to war like noir. But this
was so male, and so fallen with wordy victims. I gave up all love
that I knew of. Granted, there was a lot I did not know. I gave up
alcohol and drugs. I wish they had given me up, but this was not to
be the case. I had to give up. Then I had to give up again, when
I least expected it, and, maybe, at last. I don't know. There is still
so much I do not know.

5

When Tom died I feel now he was giving me life. He was the other man.

Tom would understand my portrait of my teeth, Langston Hughes writing

"Cora." "The ones I love."

Lonely little star. Half man.

The dream is a wage.

Moon wages.

Big Boy walks into prison like there ain't no sorrow.

One shoulders *ain't* in the dream, and the moon knows.

And the sorrow knows.

And the river knows you know, but has a lot of getting on to do.

Once you are a wave of suicide and once you are the night.

Kafka the.

Kafka Tom. Kafka Tom.

6

The Cora I knew was named Kathy in this life and she was murdered

and knifed to death when she went to the Ladies' Room and some crazed

man was waiting for his but he panicked or who knows and he knifed

Kathy to death over and over. It's taken me over thirty years to

say this let alone write this without my face slicing some. But I

won't think now Kathy ever died, not the Kathy-love. Not the word-

love. Not the lamp-love. Not the child-love. Not the heart-love.

/ Kafka-love. Too-love.

Sun-followed-by-moon-love.

Love waiting in the road.

7

In Kafka's words
one train equals one love, and
one's train equals one's love.
You see this love nameless in the city too.
And you see this love in a very hard quarrel
which creates a silence for cheap years. And creates
a traveler like rain. Nameless pictures which do not prove anything.
Pictures prove the houses were there and probably the people in them.
But abuses were exchanged too often, and you are in denial about this.
You. You. You.

Goodbye Kafka.
Goodbye kids.
Goodbye Paris.
Goodbye Art Kafka.
Goodbye Prison Counselor Kafka.
Kafka nose, Kafka mouth, Kafka eyes: goodbye

UNSLEEPING

TWO

Harlem (2)

for V.

Two copies of Jean Valentine's
The River at Wolf. I am going
to leave one by my coffee cup
for someone else to find. And
someone may see a canyon where
I see a house, and someone may
double or even triple as an angel
when the voice arrives. I am heading
on to two mesas I want to call the
moon, I am lonely to give something
back to a loser's piece of music.
I heard the someone-someone when
Henderson said don't worry, and fell
like a beginning into the wrong hotel.
Lights out, phone overdue: my husband
the cop is the story I will tell you
in the lobby but when the group of us
heads out and sees him I have to pretend
like you that I still am just a doubtful
sound.

Tooth

You did not die because of a tooth.
Not my tooth or your tooth or your mother's tooth.
Or the teeth of the neighborhood either—
the neighborhood did have teeth.
Or the mathematical tooth of the government
sending you off to another war.
Or the tooth of money which you said once
you wanted to have implanted in your brain.

Whenever we made out in the car she was sexually
erotically at ease, and this other side of her
came wildly around—she wanted me like a child
wants a dollar, like a lost son later wants rain,
like a lost tooth wants the mouth again or the root
again and the mouth knows this too and wants this
belonging back, this history back—you need to decide
with a lot less debate, less bullshit

—one time she called me by another date, another name
—we were deep inside each other and she just moaned
out this other name—I didn't say anything about it
for a long long time—maybe because I had done this
too, other times, other people, once or twice, and it
was a rare or slightly rare time where some part of me
must have been willing to say to myself she is fucking
human, give her that, so she says another name, so what

46

/ —but one time my hand was at her throat, one time she
wanted to die upside down she felt so bad for her own
life, inarticulate place where the unfolding simply
keeps going, there's no turning back, the tears are in
the throat and the teeth as well as the eyes, the neighborhood
could be called out to a fire it hurts that bad, there *is*
smoke for life's misery, and it's going to pass, and it's
going into hiding again for awhile or quite awhile.

NO

The stores lit up with their goods

—David Ignatow ("The Dream")

No purple.

No cows in the sky.

No cars in the sky with or without drivers.

No sex.

No orange (too much orange lately).

No teeth (they might bite).

No telephone unless the store is lit up and the owner is lit up

    and using the telephone (who is he calling, who does he want to rescue?

    Will the night ever be lit by the nursing of his singing? He sings,

    doesn't he? Doesn't he sing in one's mouth in the most detached way?)

No paternal grandmother.

No ace of clubs or hearts or diamonds. No seven of spades.

No pocket on yellow shirt.

No hard love or spotted rocks.

No ocean liner of cloth.

No eyeglasses to be ground into the earth by

No soldier.

No rape.

No child tormented.

No someday-old-person dismissed.

No "the rock erases no such self," uh-uh.

No no no.

No letter written to no persons unknown.

No web site without a spider.

No gate.

No proof, no ankles, no taters.

No Goose Tatum.

No Angela Skull.

No Art Tatum or Bud Powell.

No first basemen in your dream of the pedestrian city. No chair or crowd.

No stores lit up with their goods.

No friends.

No places.

No antelope at the center of the world.

No witness to the poem of a wild horse.

No September 11, 1999.

Help

Malena calls, and I am so happy
I want to pass it on; so later I call
Nancy. And in between Dave calls to tell me
he is almost finished with his painting for me,

and I forget to tell myself till now
that when Malena calls I also hear her son
Charlie in the background, and the child
in him is excited that he and his father

have had a flat tire, in the rain; and in
the first conversation with Malena Charlie
has even gotten on the telephone and talked
to me. And when I do call Nancy I hear both

Benjamin her son and Emily her daughter
moving or talking or asking for help
in the background. And much earlier in the
day Diane has called, and yesterday I called

John to wish him Happy Birthday and it did
not matter that I was two days off. And I
almost always telephone my eighty-nine-year-old
father. And the night before this Chris tells

/ me on the telephone that in Alberti's *The Lost
Grove* he begins talking about an anxiety. And
today when I look for anxiety in the book
I find a page where Rafael Alberti is expecting

a visitor from the moon, I misread/mismake
what is in the sentence for my lack of glasses.
Trying to find the page later, cannot. This
is not unlike trying to find Tomas Tranströmer's

"antibirds" in a poem. I am sure I have read
this. I tell Malena maybe antibirds do not
fly over, maybe they fly under. Malena has
been looking for something in someone's poem

also; we wonder about looking for what the other
can't find, in order to find it. But do we find
anything, ever? Dave will finish his painting,
but when will the painting be finished with him?

Someday Charlie will be in the foreground in rain.
Alberti's *Lost Grove* is like my lost friend Rusty Grove.
Not "like." You know what I mean. Words, sounds
against the sky, keep playing some part. For days

I am suffering from the flu and then a deep anxiety
sets in, or perhaps it has been there, here, in me,

simply waiting for a chance to tell me something over
many days, something I must keep missing or am still

arrogant about or closed off to, because it keeps
coming back, and one form of it is an unexpected wave
which makes the breath feel as if it will travel
somewhere else without me, which of course breath

does. And something in me is not surrendering to
sleep. I can feel this lack of surrender. Of course
it might not be anything like what I am saying, but
I wanted to say something about it, to both honor it,

or acknowledge it, or see it in words slightly outside
myself, outside my own hearing. I have also talked to
Nate about this, and Chuck, and there are many others
who have been willing to help me.

Unappreciated Butterfly

I think I was on a balcony
overlooking the whole thing.

—Yusef Komunyakaa
"April Fool's Day"

No *soon*, no hard loan, no geometric woodwork
to make you feel at home. No soap, no anonymous
bourbon, no portrait or copy of a portrait painted
by some writer or star or family member or any
other-than-artist person. No short drop
(you were fifteen floors up), no secret way
out, no voice of self-hatred (which you are at least
used to). No past tense. Sometimes no tense at all.
Sometimes not even an all or nothing. Sometimes
not even a real estate dream, not even a frame,
not even a frame*work*. A balcony but not a back
kitchen porch. A woman hanging out her laundry
but not hanging out. Railroad tracks and motor-
cycle gang around the corner but not a ticket
or a destination. Not even the sense of a weird
dead end. Not a lemon or a sun. No children.
No stories about children, no crooked arrow.
No ghost named Leslie or Vallejo. No C. No M.
No J.

You Were Locked in an Airplace

You were locked in an airplace
which felt like a snow memory.
You could escape because the day would hide itself again,
but you also knew some children were starving,
that your identity would be theirs if you remained.
Clouds, mail, airplanes near yellow light:
some of the unworldly worlds
which stayed overnight in the same airplace with you.

Now it is time to watch only the poetry
of the eyelash, the bombed street, the suitcases
belonging to the now-rich poet who adored your
writing more than a quarter of a century ago.
Blinks in time.
A quarter for your thoughts.
A quarter for your mail.
Quarter for your unmail.
Quarter for your quarters. Fuck me.

Snow looks like the light bomb in this heart.
Who are you?

You klomp along. You keep leaving letters out,
or you put one letter in front of another
like an excuse.

So long.

We Have to Talk about Another Book

The boy's glasses were very very thick.
He was thinking of this life and the next and the next.
The yellow city bus drove by the blue-by-morning river
but the boy did not see the bus from this perspective.

Two blackbirds have more space than they can handle.
No one knows time this way the way the blackbirds do.
No one knows no one: a blade of grass
is the blade in the grass. The boy stands in his ghost.

One of the blackbirds is now thick with the river.
Some of the branches make love like an awkward couple.
Or like a couple juxtaposed against the window, which
isn't unusual, but the window is juxtaposed against

branches,
and the branches are making more sounds than usual.
Things become is.
We don't have to make a sentence if we don't want to.

If My Brother Had Been a Literal Spider

Today I say to myself
If my brother had been
a literal spider he could
then put his hands all
over me—I think to
say this today, and
not try to make someone
into an artist for their
entire life or almost most
of it (my brother drew
and drew and painted and
then at sixteen gave up
this entire world and as
far as I knew the make-
believe part of it too)
—I did not want to go
this way alone. Today I
say to myself the spider
is like my brother the
artist because of its
long and many arms or
what today I will call
arms and will want them
all over me. Today I
will make use of them
I say to my brother.

Sweet Father, Sweet Moon

One watches the film unfold
—noir, the two women almost
twins, the murder making no
sense to the detective or to
the significant other of the
woman who attempted murder
(everyone is waiting for the
double-life woman to die, the
wound is that close, so I too
have already called it a mur-
der). The clothing is like
the film too: there's an ob-
long cut in the middle of MO's
dress-top which looks like a
window to the world, a window
to the half-cut moon which hangs
in space in its own space-time
directly to the eye above Venus.
One cannot take comfort always
—and falling asleep one realizes
one must leave his ninety-year-old
father now, or I will never be
able to drive back home this late.
And he misses me he says, and I
miss him. And one almost drives
back to watch the film conclude

and to say the hell with driving
back to emptiness. But one drives
on like me. Halfway home the moon
gets covered by a huge night cloud.
Venus too. The film unfolds. Noir.

A Small Window

1

The Kandinsky art book stayed in its
cellophane for three unnecessary days.
This was an opening for something, but for
what.

2

Fiction about a fiction. He had made
up the book, one suggested to the other.
It never existed. Therefore the publisher's
contract did not exist, who knows, some of
the trips to the city may have not existed
either.

3

She was actually gleeful that the possibility
of this being a fiction about a fiction
not only pleased her but made him more
appealing to her. She told her friend this
and even her friend laughed with a kind of
dull glee.

4

One writer is choosing words as if you can
constantly choose them. As if words are
a constant. To say nothing of: the space
from which seldom words choose seldom us,
or singular: he, she, you, me, I, the other
you.

5

Kandinsky's house is a giant book. No it
isn't. It doesn't look that serious, sitting
in the woods like that, trying to look serious.

6

Hughes' *The Ways of White Folks*.
You heard the word *out* today used
on the famous woman's talk show
over and over as a verb, over and
over, as if she too is trying to
impress. Forgot to ask anyone what
out means in this sense. The other
day it was

7

dis, but you misheard a *c* in it some-
where. Imagine *c* as *somewhere*, not
where it usually is, or when *c*
can be counted upon being. It is
like the

8

number in that light on Hughes'
face, and the slight mood, the
angular pitch. *C* as a sound
having a hum

9

a hundred.
"As in the lie he told me today
about the new chapter to his book
which no longer exists. He read
the same part this year at the reading
as he did last." As a part in
one *hundred*, not *one hundred*
but one *hundred*

10

he called her a name, a hundred.
he called in the middle of the day
and began to ask her serious questions
about their relationship. someone
else should have been attracted to
her by now she thought, and because
she could not feel this from anyone
new his call really agitated her even
though the call lasted only a few
minutes

11

you can be very dishonest in a very
few minutes. it does not take much
and of course i am not talking about
overt lies as i am about an angling
of lie/angles to one's self—to even
state it this way indicates the slippery
green water we have entered, i has entered
—like an R-rated version of the moon
he said. they don't mean anything
anymore: de moon, de rival, de end
of this

12

Tomas' parents were Jewish. His father,
Robert Kulka, was a businessman from the
Moravian town of Olomouc.

13

Half of Tomas' face in the photograph
taken when he was five or six or seven,
half of his face seems to know trouble
—if i cover half of it up you seem some
distant cry just slightly in the uncovered

14

behind Tomas' head and face and
young shoulders is a black backdrop
slightly angling up for half the
small 1" x 1" photograph—angled
up slightly as if Tomas is on the
deck of a boat or a ship, so the
horizon of the sea/sky line is not
straight—or the interior drape
isn't straight—small sun, simple
small

15

year, Nicole's poem, "simple small
year" she writes, she writes about
the meeting with the fortune-teller
but she knows too she is writing
about something slightly else—
life is right in front of her with
its small sun, its photograph of
Tomas, its simple small year as she
says

16

His mother, Elas Skutezka, was a
milliner from Brno, the capital of
Moravia. The couple was well-educated
and spoke both Czech and German.

17

Sometimes I thought my brother spoke
with a deck of cards—that this is
how he and my German grandmother spoke
—my Czech self looked awkwardly to
a small window

The Rearranger

I woke up this morning (or was it last night?)
and I wrote down "write something called 'The Rearranger.'"
The rearranged. The rearranger rearranging the rearranged.
The lone rearranger. Rangers of the rearranged, rearrangers
of the purple sage. The vast memory of purple. Or was it
last night when the real memory of purple recurred and recurred
like a wave? Then was gone, like a business which never opened.
Seeing a stick in the grass, a branch, maybe close to a yard long,
close to where I sat with Don when he read the letter from his lover
and his lover was writing to say he had tested positive for AIDS
and Don sitting there with a letter in his lap now, almost like
a minimal drawing of a robe from one of Mary Hackett's
drawings of the Stations of the Cross, Jesus' legs and a bearer's
hands and arms and the sense of the minimal robe to carry
or wrap Jesus in, a letter in Don's lap. A stick in the grass.
I thought I did not have any space left, but here is all this
space because of Mary's drawing and Don's lap and a stick
in the grass. Don is in the stick for a moment. I am in his lap.
Or Mary is bearing me because of all this space. I woke up
this morning and I wrote down write something called The
Rearranger.

A Small Ring

Almost all rings are small.
But this one had under its
cheap convex imitation glass
a tree, and another small
tree behind it, staggering
trees in a small picture in
a small ring in a small store
in a small not-even town in
a time when you yourself were
much smaller than you felt,
about to enter more phases
of life unawares, blind to
what you're doing really,
people you are about to hurt,
ghost of yourself you are to
hurt again, and you are also
missing lives of course you
could have helped in small
ways, lives which needed help,
—people claim people like
objects, what's the use, al-
most all people are small
when it come to claim-time.

See Seascape (September)

My box and my foot is up. Where are you?

Big basket, smaller hat. Cigarettes, bicycle.

When you die you live like a Christmas tree.

Plain box. Plain white sun as she was plain white sun.

Increase in some kind of other said.

Proposition to rain. At learning. Broke my eye.

My tongue is not the conspiracy of horizon.

My foot and my by.

Buy me a gift before I buy you one.

One story is you never liked me.

Me has no d.

Me has everything breath does not have.

"If you got a diamond ring it meant the relationship was over."

(Langston)

It begins with atonement as if upon a train.

Georg whispers Rachel.

All simple cruelties.

Sleds banging in the wind in the fierce woods.

Tree (2)

That sound not there. Wrong to the very door.

Discussed lights. "All with me."

Birdbath. Weeping. Me is, me is stung by a bee.

I am sorry but your face is a close wave.

Real sea. Nobody. A nobody. Anti-not.

Real sea. Anti-bodice.

Real see. Anti-nobody.

Lucky I did not have I have real sea. Buy shot to anti-knot.

We were driving down the road and all around.

We knew we were near the artist's lane who had died.

We knew this was near the lane we embarrassingly took before.

Life you meant.

You meant life. Not after that kiss, word—

Ice cream. Lightning. I found your.

Box angel (city)

Moon Thief

Someone stole the moon tonight. It wasn't me. It wasn't you.
It wasn't the snow because the snow had already fallen.

Someone stole the moon tonight and maybe it's in my room.
Behind the mask. Which is empty and hanging from the doorknob.

Someone stole the moon tonight and emptiness could hide it.
Is your room an emptiness like night can be? How about day?

I don't think the mask is less of a mask for not having a face
behind it.

Snow is still snow. Are you waiting for me to tell you I am
waiting for the snow to tell me what else it is?

This is beginning to upset me.
And when the snow had always already fallen, a little ways up

the street in a small cemetery, always beneath the feet of a woman
in a statue—when the snow had always already fallen

I was living with a woman who did not know where I walked nor did
she know the invisible people I talked to when I walked

(this took place, though it surprises me to be so honest,
almost always during daytime. As if night or even evening rendered

70

invisible people useless, or (that sounds too cruel to me)—or
at least gone or not hearing).

Because she did not know whom I spoke with or where I walked I
probably did not give us much of a chance. Because these were

very important moments and voices for me, underestimated even
by myself. And sometimes the glass bottles and glass shapes I

would see through ground level or slightly below windows—well
these were telling me a lot about *something*, and I was in no hurry

to know just what, I will let them determine that, although I was
in a stupid hurry with just about everything else in my life at the

time because it seemed important to impress people and keep going.
Very foolish. Very stupid, to give up her and *something* for that.

But most of all I wanted to tell you or want to tell you now that
one of those impressed probably took some of my writing off the floor

one night and did who knows what to it, maybe just kept it, like a
corpse, like bones, who knows—I myself had thrown the stuff down

enraged by how my life was getting completely out of my own hands
and I could see or tell (but only silently and in some truly hidden

corner which guarantees you don't see or tell anything to anyone,
including your poorer and poorer self)—I could see I was not headed

in any direction which would have me reaching out and being responsible
for my own life. It was too late for that, at least not now, not

for anything would I truly give up. So life was a mess. But what
I think of now is that stealing those writings I had thrown down

is like someone stole the moon tonight. It wasn't me. It wasn't you.
It wasn't the snow because the snow had already fallen.

But I wanted to find a way back to you. Like the moon.
And this seemed as good as any.

Face in a Train Window

The small mountain rises like a gumdrop of snow.
Two small creeks before the train crosses the township.
I want to live here and here and here, at the blue house
which hobbles the plain houses leading to it—so blue
a traveler like me would eat the house
and the other
yellow one as the train leaves town.

I want to live there and there and there
if I had grown up in that town. I would have stared
at the train traveling to another life, stared for a face
in a train window, a face which would carry my spirit with it
or depart from the train in the next town, return until it found me
to steal me to the other
—if I grew here I would still want to eat the blue house and the yellow house.

Another small mountain rises like another gumdrop of snow.
Hear my mother talking. "About three minutes to eight. Two minutes.
Something like that."
The refusal to say the definitive, the simple, the brief, the clear:
did my difficulty in this derive at all from my mother? What did I hear,
how did I hear it?

I want to bring you here in a condition like silence.
Do not let me talk.
The houses talk, the spruces talk, today across the world is listen-

to-a-tree-talk day, I could tell from how they dripped in the rain
with snow still deep around them.

This next town consists of houses hidden along the river
and a few thousand leaves which never even fell.

Weather

to Jo and Ed

When I used to stay at my brother's
I would turn once a visit inside a
book called *Weather* and look for the
green and dark green and whitish and
little yellow little drawing of what
was intended to be a parent and a child
walking in the rain under an umbrella.
It was a place from the place nobody
minded and the rain could remind me
that I would be back at my brother's
again, even if it was a world I resisted
or wanted to resist. Because I would
have to sleep on the couch even after
all these years, and it was the same
couch even after all these years, and
notes and objects and formulae from
the past and the family past would always
give me a tinge of suffocation, if only
just at first. Until the second night,
when so tired from teaching and everyone
else's agendae during a day I would be
glad I only had to drive nine miles before
driving another two hundred and seventy
"home." And my brother would not be
asking for much if anything at all, and

I would be on the couch knowing I had
a slight feel for why blood is thicker
than water. And I ended this unexpectedly
even for myself, and was sort of stunned
for years for having given up this job.
Probably because I had something off
or wrong somewhere about my mother or
my brother or my blood or my teaching.

Unsleeping

What could you call this? The house we enter?
Days. Dreams. Roads with snow, black ice, high forest,
despite civilization, still to the side.
But the house we enter gives each of us a language,
a translation; each can either leave the world behind
the house, or help the world enter, or help the house
enter the solemn or not-so-solemn world.

But tonight you realize someone, or someones, or somethings,
images, misgivings—any one or more of these as places—
tonight you realize someone taught you it was safest, easiest,
to say I am sick, or I do not feel well, or I am ill, to say these
as the only surefire words which the people in your house will hear
and honor and thus leave you alone.
I am a postcard of snow and you are my footstep.

This surefire would be harmless enough unless one begins to realize
and almost like trees or proofs count the endless countless times
one has a chance to utter these, and all the more so as you are not
truly aware that it is these words which you are using for nets
for your house and your language and your translation and your
people. Because I do not feel well I guess I will not travel
to the lighthouse with you this afternoon. Thank you.

Blue: if you don't mind I will remain in the house. Something's
wrong. I'm not feeling well. To il postino: please do not deliver

mail tomorrow. I have, as you have probably suspected, a weakness
somewhere in my body. Have you ever felt it? I am touched by it.
My childhood is not metal but I know the frame of my face no longer
has the feel of the moon. And on another side of the room my brother
is so chronological it hurts.

When one lyric dies replace it with another.
Do not ever un me again.
Get out of this soap before I meet you in the forest.
Free A.
Free me.
The house we enter turns to page 134.
It is even longer and another side to say page one hundred and thirty-
four. But in that length it is possible to lose breath if your breath
is already lost, or almost lost.
Lately my breath has been almost lost.
If there is any possibility she loved me like A. loved me, it makes
perfect sense that less than nothing was said about that feeling or
that possibility. It makes more sense that things happened and were
vocalized as they were: words were things which moved from her in a
backward direction at times, and often the words were on the other side
of things. This is not unlike how A. was manhandled by the government.
It is also not unlike how I speak also. How I lyricize. How I vocal.
How you vocal is up to you and the translations of the various houses
you have chosen to enter. Some of us, like A., had no choice but were
shoved into this room or that night or this train or this lyric. And
some, unlike A., did not come out at any side at all. Nor as a part
of any voice. Nor as a part of any vocal. Unless words were things

which also moved backwards from them at times, and often the words were
on the other side of things they had been forced to leave behind.
Snow do not leave me.
A. do not leave me, or leave me a word.
Getting out of this soap before I meet you in the forest takes on new
meaning.
I love it when people like myself think something has taken on new
meaning. I love it, but I do not trust it.
But I am not sick any longer nor will I say so and I will enter a
house and I will also look for A.

You are knowing a star. It has come from a vocal.
The part of snow which is unchildhood.

Whenever I know my sister has left the world with this other
older man, I know she has entered a slightly different house.
My brother and I are so isolate perhaps we two are also in different
houses. It would not seem so but I cannot pretend to know. I
say this not to be critical, but to allow my own sense of my own
you to talk more clearly, even if the images flatten against space
or supposed space. This is not unlike my father's still voice,

this supposed space, and I do not mean this as a voice from childhood
or youth or nostalgia, but rather a voice which is one side. Equivocal
time, you who are there against the window as a passerby. You must
recede because you are sick and although they cannot find anything
wrong with you you must if necessary now lie in order to guarantee
your place in the harbor of the world. And then develop a disease

in a true sense, unknown to you as it develops, not unlike men of
action in the western democracies develop sympathy. How many A.'s
have been murdered by trees instead of men? I remember the night and
the equivocal train against the night and against the vocal of the night.
As you slept an air mile or two from the sound of the train and the
vocal of the train. And you also would unsleep to this, which is not
quite like awakening because you were not quite sleeping yet, neither
were you drifting. You were unsleeping in the vocal of the train.
It is 1954 but this is not a view from childhood. It is a view from
your sister and the coal of your sister who had no childhood. It is
an unreverie and an unchildhood if you must know. But you must know
that much less than knowing A., who was being shipped on a small train,
on a same train, on a same time, on a same vocal, to some school almost
prison in Oklahoma because A. had done bad and was being moved from
one family and one tribe to another. The vocal of A. who tells you his
train some forty years after you unvocal it. Your sister who does not
know nor hear A. knows more of A. than you do.

The house you enter may be your own but it sounds more like A.'s house.
The snow is deep in sleep and the land has been taken from the snow.

have this dream

have this dream
wherein i am making
connection to woman
and man whom i used

to know and i have
finally stopped at
their house to be
with them again if

only for a few minutes
of course i don't know
how i will be received
what a strange word

received
what a strange idea
really
to go to their house

like this it's even
stranger that i am
willing to do this
in a dream it would

make more sense to
do this in the daily
waking life i will
get back to you

i will let you know
how and when i was
received

House

More time than I'm willing to
admit or be afraid of. Less

a house than a cloud where
a sick neighborhood cat can

reside. Less a door than a
weight a student miscalculates.

More time to telephone light,
to wait for the hook of your

next appointment. To see you
standing next to the lamp

of the panther—to see you
snow, hourglass. Rumors.

Why Night

Why night to ever
be without such
wonderful abundance
as you brought to
sea

Notes about My Face

1

Traces. Then things themselves are not names
not words only.

2

Hay. I am not hay.
I am not hey either.
My mother meant one of these. Or both.

3

Both moons in one month.
Both rains on Tuesday.
Both cold snows on 5.

4

Reaching for the salt:
a) she is stabbed by the father
b) she is stabbed by the father's fork
c) she is stabbed by the father's father
d) hello. she is inside

5

"I miss myself
in the earlier version"
I write to Jean.

6

"interesting"—1 of my mask words

7

she is inside:
                "I" wrote

to literal companion of
mine in literal light
on "porch-stage" (Jean's)
of 1968, the summer the

New Yorker published a
translation by Babel's daughter
of "You Must Know Everything"
—and Jane Flory read it

aloud in the back evening
—and Sheldon Flory took
notes about my face during
this and put them in a

poem—

or so

it

seems

then—Jean Valentine's small
"porch-stage..."
"ghost guide..."
i became "I" at some pivot
in this place ⎯⎯⎯→ arrow
                 is the

                    face of,

face of

No rearranged rider.
No ghost behaviors.
No umbrella.

8

"too much glass" K's
translation of T reads
—one thinks of one's own
house or house past or
room as having too much
too—but one is silent

/ no recovery artist

no box of recovery

the boys in the basement

are shattered in the skull

and in the heart—in the

cases

9

of these two murders by

the father the heart is

equal in size to the shattered

skull and the shattered window

10

and in at least 6 other moments

on this globe this appropriate word

globe for this earth at at least

6 other moments there are equal

murders—the word daily cannot

convey this—the broken branch

on 16th Street two Novembers ago

is the link to the moment of one

of the two deaths

11

your honor
my thesis will be based
upon Myung Mi Kim's DURA
and Duras' Two by Duras
The Atlantic Man
The Slut of the Normandy Coast
a new world

12

how to refer to these two (Two)
will be the initial pivot
and probably final pivot

feeble insomnia
brick of the school

13

the elementary school
in e elementary evening

14

something like candy cities
—"*Waipo* stands for maternal grandma. *Wai* means 'outside,'
'stranger.' *Po*, 'old woman.'"   (Wang Ping, "Female Marriage")

/ I want my Maypo.
outside means no snow
outside means stolen drawing from snow's friend
outside means Jean Valentine's "ghost guide"

    15
I had this feeling
        Sheldon was up
to something, Jane too—

maybe not Jane, maybe not Jean
—sometimes, from Jean's incredible
poem Ironwood

sometimes I thought I was
"the other Michael"—
            I asked her
last November, finally,
after wanting to ask for

a long time, and she sort
of said she could not recall
who that was—were we walking
along arm in arm

after she gives this wonderful

reading of poems from this

book she is now thinking (May)

of calling HER LOST BOOK.

I don't believe her, about "the other

Michael," but it becomes vague now

like a snowy fact, like some of

the most interesting facts in poems

do—mask facts

literal light:

16

LAMB

| cuban

| panther

JASPER JOHNS—ANXIETY—A MAN WHO WANTED ME BUT I
   WAS WRONG

Street of pain

Someone is actually going to pay me to hang out in churches

"I don't want an adversarial relationship c̄ my writing, you have"

Don't sleep with your head in the sun here

"I COME FROM SECRETS"   John Frazier

have told our dog a dog we had another dog we had a story we should not

LATIN   "His friends did not see him for months."

too much house too much wind in the sense of wind against trees and house

The liability of the inside

Kim's "Large pond gives way"

Kim's Collect the years' duration

"AND YEARS AGO, TOO"   Melissa Hotchkiss   Could *not* see the
    ball coming

said his brother, and the rain helped the silent father understand his silence

again: the songs

little did you know i almost threw myself under the train tonight

little did you know

people claim people like objects

today the story of my friend the sea. Tomorrow, utter sexuality of the sea

YOU PROBABLY WON'T STEAL FROM YOUR MOTHER IN LAW
    AGAIN FOR A WHILE

i was intimidated by weldon kees

painted digression 8500 ghosts today painted senators with money bags
    for faces

painted representatives with blades for ears painted soldiers with assholes

for brains painted murderers with US painted all over their hearing

painted punishments for another woman   painted brutality for another
    child

evening coast loan sudden reverse far scamper duck globe refrain to
    per drop

see my difficult gone he talked part door she broughtnightly crows

this bird was a sign or not unhate the hand the pelvis   hello blue moon

Notes

The next-to-last line of "The Thanker" is indebted to the poem "Portents" by Sheldon Flory, from his book *A Winter's Journey* (Copper Beech Press, Providence, 1979). The last line of "Portents" reads "Loneliness, the beast, the blind snow."

In "A Small Window," parts 12 and 16 are from Tomas Kulka's *Identification Card (#6742)* from the United States Holocaust Memorial Museum.

Many of these poems owe their existence to stories-in-part from friends, and tones from friends and music and art. I am sure I am unintentionally forgetting some people, but I would like to thank very much Mary Alice Johnston, Dave Ackerman, Robert Wald, Nancy Modlin Katz, Diane Wald, Malena Mörling, my brother Peter Allen Burkard, Nancy Mitchell, Nicole Greenwood, Rod Ladousier, Grace Paley, John Fitzpatrick, Michael Gervasio, Tomas and Monica Tranströmer, Lisa Bateman, Chris Kennedy, Cindy Roberts, Catherin Gammon, Tess Gallagher, my sister Elizabeth Casazza, John Skoyles, Maria Flook, Kim Wahle, Ed Ruchalski, JoEllen Kwiatak, Jo Ann and Charlie Freer, Michael Paul Thomas, James Wagner, Vincent Standley, Shreerekha Pillai, Arielle Greenberg, Rob Morris, and Giannina Braschi.

I would also like to thank Arthur Vogelsang for his editorial support over many years, and a thanks to Sarah Gorham and Jeffrey Skinner for the arrangement of the contents of this book.

A special thanks to Jean Valentine and Sheldon Flory, poets whose work has lived with me for many years.

I would also like to thank my father, Paul Burkard, and a thanks, in memoriam, to Leslie Cook, Don Sterton, Mary Hackett, and my mother, Ashley Brittain Burkard.

The Author

Michael Burkard teaches in the MFA Writing Program at Syracuse University and at the Fine Arts Work Center in Provincetown. He has received prizes from *The American Poetry Review* and the Pushcart Press. He has received fellowships from the Fine Arts Work Center at Provincetown, the National Endowment for the Arts, and the New York Foundation for the Arts. His books of poems include *The Fires They Kept* (Metro Book Co., 1986), *My Secret Boat* (W.W. Norton, 1990), and *Entire Dilemma* (Sarabande, 1998). He lives in Syracuse, New York.

Nancy Mitchell